To all my parents out there who are truly listening remember it's a small step, not a sprint and your kid is unique in his or her own unique way. If you're truly listening to these words, I promise you, you will tap into something special and you will see progress in your child's sports journey, much faster, and much quicker than you think. It's not a football. It's not a basketball. It's not a softball that will make your child great. It's not anything it's you the parent that controls your kids' destiny and that can propel your child forward. You can either propel them into their destiny or you can hinder them in their destiny. I hope this book helps you propel your kid in the right direction and just remember, trust the process, and enjoy the journey and every second of every moment of your child because tomorrow's not promised. You are not alone, I'm doing the same. It's just work with tons of love.

-Jamal Merrell

Hello, my name is Jamal Merrell. I started playing sports at the age of 6. Today, I'm 32 and now on the other side as a sports parent. From experience, I've learned this side is challenging, and I've learned things that I want to pass on to you; we will HIT KEY POINTS THAT WILL HELP YOU as a sports parent and even better you as a parent.

SPORTS PARENT BOOK

JAMAL MERRELL

Sports Parent Book

By Jamal Merrell

Cover Created by: Jamal Merrell

Logo Design: Justin Ackerman and Angel Jones

Editor: Anelda Attaway

© 2024 Jamal Merrell

ISBN 978-1-954425-98-9

All rights reserved. This book is protected under the copyright laws of the United States of America. This book may not be copied or reprinted for commercial gain or profit. The use of short quotations or occasional page copying for personal or group study is permitted and encouraged. Permission will be granted upon request for Worldwide Distribution, available in Paperback. Printed in the United States of America. Published by Jazzy Kitty Greetings Marketing & Publishing, LLC. Dba Jazzy Kitty Publications is utilizing Microsoft Publishing Software.

DEDICATIONS

This book is dedicated to my children Aslyn and Jamal, without whom this book would never be completed, I love you both and I appreciate all the many lessons, and may we continue on this sports journey together. I love you both from the bottom of my heart SO MUCH NO MATTER WHAT. I think the best thing a person can be in this world is a great parent. I can say with pride that I'm damn good at it. Being a father to you both is the best thing that I could ever be on this earth. I will continue to be the man and father who loves, cares, teaches, and guides you through this journey called life.

To my parents Benny and Darlene who have allowed me to grow in the sports world and taught me so many lessons while growing up.

Also to my brother Jamil and BJ who was my rider and with me along every step of my sports journey while growing up and always pushing me to be elite.

Thank you to my incredible wife for being my best friend, motivator, and encourager. You've not only supported me, but you've also taught me invaluable lessons on parenthood and our journey through our kids' sports. Thank you for letting me become the person that I'm always becoming. Thank you for giving me that look during games that says stop it loud and clear. Thank you for holding my hand during games you know I'm ready to grab a clipboard and go replace the existing coach, you've been there every step of the way. Watching our kids grow through their sports alongside you is one of the most fulfilling experiences I've ever had. I love you so much no matter what."

ACKNOWLEDGMENTS

Thank you for enabling me to overcome the challenges I once found daunting. I'm grateful for introducing my best friend into my life, who is now my spouse. In moments of darkness, you showed me the way. Thank you for instilling in me the drive to push harder even when I had all I needed. Amidst difficulties, you've allowed me to maintain happiness and wear a constant smile. When adversity stares me down, I stand firm, fortified by your guidance. You've shaped me into the person I am today, navigating through all that has transpired. Thank you for as my circle got smaller you remained constant in my life.

Thank you, God.

TABLE OF CONTENTS

INTRODUCTION i

CHAPTER 1 – Verbal Communication 01

CHAPTER 2 – Scoreboard 06

CHAPTER 3 – Actions 07

CHAPTER 4 – Humble Them 11

CHAPTER 5 – Quiet 12

CHAPTER 6 – Resources 15

CHAPTER 7 – Environment 20

CHAPTER 8 – Conclusion 22

ABOUT THE AUTHOR 23

INTRODUCTION

I began playing sports at the age of 6 years old. Sports has taught me many valuable things, and they have allowed me to visit great cities and states across the U.S.

Today, I'm a husband, father of two (girl and boy), former collegiate three-year starter and captain in football, state trooper, mentor, and former National Football League player. This is not an exhaustive list—just some of the things that I have been involved with and accomplished in my life. From playing sports for so long and knowing all the ins and outs, my biggest challenge now is not being on the field but being on the sidelines watching my kids.

Being a sports parent and being in the stands is a completely different atmosphere; one that many don't realize plays a huge role in your kids' sports development. I have come up with seven important tips that I've learned and developed over the years that have not only made me a better sports parent but, most importantly, a better father and husband.

These seven tips will not only help fathers but also any sports parent or family member who plays a large role in a child's life by attending sports. These tips are only my opinions, based on what I've experienced and learned over time, but trust me, when

I look at my kids today, I know that, mentally and physically, they can move mountains with a smile while they are playing sports.

CHAPTER 1

VERBAL COMMUNICATION

When it comes to sports, verbal communication can go a long way. As a sports parent, start by encouraging everything your kid does well, from jumping, sliding, passing, dribbling, tackling, and swimming to whatever it is they are succeeding at or trying to attempt in their sport. Whatever it is that your child does well, tell them Good job; do it consistently.

Some key phrases to say in any sport are "Good job," "Good try," "Way to hustle," "Keep your head up," or, "Good job, I see you out there!" Remember, you as a parent may have many years of experience in a particular sport, but your child does not. Know that while learning or trying to attempt something in sports, your child will try to impress you and only you. Saying good job as a parent goes a long way to acknowledging that.

Do not be that parent who only yells at your child during a game when he or she makes a mistake. I'll say that again: do not be a parent whom your kid hears talking or yelling only when he or she makes a mistake. Trust me, in that case, your kid will be the one in the locker room who says, "Man, I wish my parent was not here." During your child's game, they will be trying to mentally focus. If they are only hearing your voice during their mistakes, then you as a parent are only creating more stress for your child. This stress will bleed over into future games, and your child will be thinking, "Is my dad here? Is my mom here?" because they will be trying to prepare themselves for the negative stress you add.

Parents, you must understand, that your child's nerves and mind will be racing because they want to do everything right to win the game or even just to play in the game. You don't want that feeling to double for your child because of worry of having to hear your voice in a negative aspect during the game. Don't get me wrong: for sure, be your kids' biggest fan. Just understand that when your kid makes a mistake they will know it, and calling out their mistake in a negative way will not only add stress but will also broadcast their mistake to the entire crowd. Sitting at my kids' games, I hear some parents yell things like, "You're killing me! You could've made it, come on, hustle, run!" I never hear any words of encouragement from those parents during the game.

Please, allow your kids to hear you when they do well. Whether it's for something big or small, let them hear and see you showing encouragement in a positive way rather than hearing you during the negative times. I can think back to many games of mine where I would hear my parents yelling, "Good job," and when I looked in the stands, I could see them clapping and smiling. Hearing and seeing the energy and love coming from my parents gave me more energy, which motivated me to play harder. Over time, that positive energy is what helped me to become a tremendous athlete and a leader and captain of every team I ever played on. As a parent now watching my daughter play basketball, I know that when she misses a shot and she hears me yell, "Come on baby, you should've made that," she processes that as, "Oh man, my dad just yelled at me." She now not only feels the pressure of missing but of me as her dad yelling at her about what she just did. The next time my daughter comes down to shoot the ball, if she misses, without me even saying a word she will automatically process that negatively, like, "My dad is mad at me for that second one"—even if I didn't say anything from the stands. This is where I caution parents: yelling negativity at your child can turn into verbal abuse without you as a parent even knowing it. I understand this because I used to fall victim to being the parent in the stands always yelling when my kid made a mistake. I'll never forget the time my wife looked at me during my kid's game and said, "Babe, you're yelling every time she messes up! Let her go, she will fix it, be quiet!" Hearing, "Be quiet" made me so frustrated, but I realized my wife was right and I was the wrong one. From then on, I knew I had to take that step back and just be quiet.

Over time, by remaining quiet after my daughter made a mistake, I could see her glance over as if she was thinking, "Is my dad even here" because I was silent. I began to observe that after my daughter made a mistake, she would focus more on fixing it rather than getting in her own head and worrying about me yelling at her. Trust me, this wasn't easy, and it took some time, but I wanted the best for my kid. So, over time, I turned my child's mistakes into a positive by yelling words of encouragement. Today, my daughter sees me standing up and clapping and hears me yelling, "Good job, baby, let's go!" I know she might feel a little bit embarrassed from the energy and love I'm showing, but she sees that I'm happy and hears me when she makes or misses a shot. It's called positive reassuring.

Today, my kids will hear me positively reassuring them when they do something good 100% more when they make a mistake. If you can do this, you will see your kid's confidence increase because they have one less thing to worry about. Trust me, I get it; as a parent, you want to yell and support your kids, but just be mindful of what is it you're yelling. What changed me was that I listened to my son and daughter after their games more than anything. Over time, I learned that for the games when my daughter didn't perform her best and that I constantly was yelling in, she would partially blame me. Thinking back to those games, I realized that after the game, my daughter used to get in the car and not say a word to me. Not only was she hurt from losing the game, but also, she was even more hurt by how she constantly heard her father in a negative tone after every mistake. Then, as a father, I would try to rebuild her—but at that moment, it was too late; the damage had been already done.

I learned to encourage in my highest tone with good energy. When my daughter makes a mistake, I use the same good-energy tone but with more encouraging words, like "All good," "You ok," "Get the next one baby," and "Get it back." Now when getting into the car, I see a smile, and my daughter wants to talk to me about the game. My kid's having fun: that's the bigger picture.

CHAPTER 2

SCOREBOARD

D o not preach to your kid that he or she didn't score enough points. Trust me: if you're this parent, you're failing your kid. Your high demand will cause your kid to check the scoreboard in the middle of the game. This can cause your kid to have a me, me, me attitude because you, the parent, are putting a score number-target on their back. Then if they don't reach that score, whether they had a good game or not, he or she will be discouraged. This ultimately takes the fun out of the game.

Parents, trust the process: listen to each step and truly follow them. You will see your kids' actions and scores go up, and ultimately, they will be having fun doing it, which is the best outcome of them all. Remember, you're not the coach, so don't act like one from the stands.

CHAPTER 3

ACTIONS

LOVE. Show your kid love, not only through wins but more through losses. If your kid wins the game, great! Take them out to eat, hug them after the game, or develop a special handshake—these are great ways for you to build a better connection with your kid and make your kid feel good inside. After a loss or bad game, don't be that parent who shows your love by talking the whole car ride home about what your kid could've or should've done. Trust me, if your kid is truly into that sport, he or she will understand what they did wrong, and they don't need you reiterating something they already know. This type of behavior can cause your kid to go into depression before they even leave the locker room because they not only know they messed up in the game but also, they still have to deal with their mother or father in the car and mentally replay the game. So, I caution you, just watch that, and then show a lot of love after the game.

Some parents don't know how to show love. I see some parents after games walking with their kids and talking about everything that their kids did wrong. No matter the outcome of any game or whatever happened during it, when it's done, a simple action that all parents can do is give their child a hug, high-five, or even just hold their hand during the walk to the car.

To me, the biggest action that all parents can do is just be present. A lot of parents think they need to show love in the most loving ways, like kisses and hugs all the time. That stuff is fine, but the number one way I show love to my kids is by just being present. I see a lot of kids out there working hard in games, and no parent is there watching him or her. I also see a lot of kids looking into the stands for their mom and dad. Being present is enough. You don't have to say a word. I'll say that again: if you are just present, you don't have to say a word. Just you being there is enough love for your kid—it will go a long way. If your kid is too young and doesn't understand it now, as they grow up, they will understand and love you that much more knowing that "Wow, my mom or dad was present. They watched me be great. They watched me grow into the athlete I am today." So just be present.

To the parents out there that can't be present: I get it. It's okay. All you need to do is put in the time and effort. If you know the parents of another kid who plays on the same team as your child, make a call and ask what the final score was. You can ask how your kid did, so when you do get home or you do finally make it to pick your kid up after the game, you can have that conversation: "The score was 58 to 50, y'all won by eight!" Your child may know you weren't there, but they'll feel much more reassured knowing that you took the time to find out the score. You can even make it into a joke, like "I'm everywhere! "Something as simple as making a phone call to find out a little information is enough to show your child you care enough to know that they made a big shot during the game or simply that you know the final score. Trust me, not being there and not knowing anything can play a huge factor. Remember parents, it only takes one phone call or one click online to follow a game play-by-play.

Outside of sports, let your kid be a kid and have fun. Do not link or compare everything to sports. If you're this type of parent, I caution you that there is a high chance that when your kid reaches higher level sports (high school, college, pros), they will be mentally done with everything involving that sport. Some of the best athletes today are not playing at the pro level because they're mentally drained and done with it from all the mental abuse and mental limits put on them throughout their childhood. Most just want to live life. From this mental sports trauma, some young athletes turn to drugs and alcohol as they reach adulthood from all the pressure that they're dealing with from sports. Don't push your kids into these paths of destruction.

CHAPTER 4

HUMBLE THEM

Whatever sport your kid plays, they will see the best of the best and watch them dance and celebrate on YouTube and television. Your child may try to act like that particular person, but yet they still stumble over their own two feet. Let them know that they're not there yet and have a long way to go. Let them hear it takes a lot of work to get to a particular level. Use it as a teaching point.

My son loves to watch videos of Tyreek Hill, an NFL receiver. During my son's football games, my son tries to dance after a two-yard gain. To humble my son every now and then, I tell him, "Tyreek can dance after he scores because he knows he ran full speed to outrun everyone. If you want to dance, do it in the end zone, but you have to outrun everyone first, like Tyreek." I use what my son likes to watch to my advantage as a parent. and it helps. Since my son likes to dance and imitate Tyreek Hill, after I humbled him, he ran his tail off to do his dances. In all, he is learning and is getting better during the process.

CHAPTER 5

QUIET

You have to know when to be quiet as a sports parent. If you're a parent who does not put in the time or give your kid the resources to be great for that particular sport, then at all games, you should be the quietest.

Going to youth or high school games, I notice that the loudest parents are the ones whose kids never do training sessions or only know the bare minimum of the fundamentals. And still, they are the ones yelling at the refs to make the calls. If you're that parent, you deserve to be the quietest one in the gym or in the stands.

On the other hand, there are some parents who do put their kids in sports training, and they know their kids put in the work. This is the category I fall into.

I am fortunate that I've played sports since I was 6, and now I can pass all that knowledge down to my kids, but I fall victim to this as well, having once been the parent at all games yelling, "Come on baby, you should've made that! Come on let's go! Pick it up! Go up strong!" Not to mention that if a referee made a bad call or didn't call something, I would be the first to let them know "Come on ref!" "You didn't see that, ref!?" "Ref, I know you saw that!" "That was not a foul!" In most games, you could hear me before the coaches even got out a word. My wife, sitting next to me, would tap my leg, which meant babe shut it, be quiet.

Learning to overcome this talking and yelling from the sideline was one of the most frustrating learning curves for me. Having played sports my entire life hinders me because when you know the game, you develop a sixth sense and can see things before they happen; or, knowing plays, you may yell who to pass the ball to because you see the mismatch. What helped me the most was beginning to tell myself, "You're not the coach." Also, over time, my wife and parents advised me to coach, so that's what I did.

Simple: If you're not the coach, don't act like a coach, but if you can't stop acting like the coach, then go be a coach somewhere.

I caution you, if your kid is getting the training, and you know your kid is putting in the time, sometimes you have to be quiet, because who is the one voice that your kid hears? It's you, the parent. Yours is the one voice that, no matter what the coaches or fans say, your kids will hear over them all. There could be 10,000 people in the stands, but that one voice that your kid hears is yours, no matter if it's good or something bad.

All sports parents must know when to be quiet. When I

learned when to be quiet, I noticed my son and daughter tapped into a higher level of play because the one voice they could hear, my voice, was a lesser distraction and didn't add any stress.

CHAPTER 6

RESOURCES

Seek knowledgeable outside training. Find someone who has experience in your child's particular sport, not someone who's never done it. Sports parents, listen to me when I say this: seeking outside resources for your kids is great, but please seek outside training for your kids from somebody who has done the sport that your kid is playing and wants to learn more about. There are millions of athletic trainers out there. Trust me when I tell you this. This is where some parents fall victim because they don't know what they don't know. Some parents don't have the knowledge; they just pick a local trainer. Parents, please do your research. If the trainer has never played the sport that you're trying to help your kid improve in, please find another trainer.

There are a lot of different specific trainings out there, like weight training, speed training, athlete body training, sport-specific training, and many more. If the price is right, it's a local trainer, and that's your only option and you have to go with it, that's fine. Just make sure you do your research because if you can drive the extra mile or pay the extra $5 or $20 to get your kid that training with a trainer experienced in your child's sport, then please hire that particular trainer.

The trainer with no experience in the sport your child is playing will only hinder your kid from getting better mentally and physically. Yes, that trainer can tell your kid to do some drills or do some workouts, that's fine. But when it all comes down to it, if your kid asks, "OK, well in the game how do I do that?" Ask yourself as a parent, is that trainer truly giving your kid the best answer?

On the flip side, if my kid has a trainer with experience in the sport my kid is doing, and while doing a drill my son stops to ask, "How does this drill help me in the game?" Hands down, that trainer who has experience will be able to answer that question in the way your kids will understand, such as "Well, in the game, if somebody's running to you and you're running towards the right, you'll be able to do this drill, break it down with your right foot just like we're doing, and as you plant with that right foot you can push your body to the left exactly how we're doing in his drill to make the defender miss." Now my son has not only processed the drill physically but processed the drill mentally because that trainer was able to break it down exactly and show how the drill will transfer to the game in a real-life situation. Parents trust me this goes a long way.

There are too many trainers out there who do not have a clue how to play the sport, yet they're training kids in that sport. Please tell me how far that will go, and I'm telling you it will not. With a trainer with experience, you not only will get your money's worth, but I guarantee you your kid will not only benefit physically but mentally as well. That trainer will build them up in ways that a trainer that never played a sport cannot. This is just my opinion, but having grown up playing football, when I train kids I not only can train them but I'm giving them the training tips and reasons why I pick certain drills and how they can apply these drills in the games. Also, having experience, I only do training drills that I know will help them in the long run and that will transfer to the game. This style of training correlates directly to the game. After all, I know what works because I did it, and I know it works. I know what does not work.

If you as a parent don't really know, then you won't know what you don't know. Now you will. All parents say they want the best for their kids. If you truly want the best for your kid and you seek outside training for your kid, at some point, don't be scared to ask that trainer, "Have you ever played a sport, and, if so, which one?" Also ask, "How can you make my daughter or son better in this particular sport?" Ask what type of training is their strong suit.

Know this, all trainers have a particular skill and something they love to focus on, such as drills, strength training, or stretching. Just think about this, parents: there is a huge difference between a trainer saying, "Do this, do that" and a trainer who has done the sport or played the sport or made it to a high level in that sport. That trainer is not saying, "Do this, do that," they're saying, "This is why you do that," and giving a reason from experience that will give your kid a real-life example of why they are doing that particular drill. Trust me this plays a huge factor in your kids' mental and physical athletic development. Think of it like this, parents: if you own a Lamborghini, would you let a person who never received their license drive it? That is the same mindset you have to have with your child's training. Having played a sport and having experience is the license.

Remember parents, there are NO EXCUSES. Don't be the parent saying your kid is not blessed with athlete genetics, or it's not in them, or you don't have the time to make your child better. There are plenty of great trainers out there for high or cheap prices, and even some who will work with your child for free. You have to do the research. I will make it even easier on you: if all else fails, there are plenty of free training videos on YouTube that don't cost a dime. Take your child to an open field, press play on the YouTube training video, and boom—let your child follow along.

Listen to me when I say this, and please don't let it fly over your head. All great sports trainers at some point posted a video of them training clients. Also, all great athletes for your child's particular sport have posted to social media videos of them training at some point. Whether it's on YouTube, Instagram, or Facebook, you will be surprised, all you have to do is find it because it's readily accessible.

CHAPTER 7

ENVIRONMENT

We all want the best for our kids, so do your part and take your kid around athletes who are already doing the sport that your child is doing. As an example, take your child to local youth games. Youth games will allow your child to not feel pressure because they're not playing and they can relax, watch, and take everything in. Also, in youth sports, there are a lot of corrections that can be seen from the stands. This will help your child to grow mentally. For example, at a basketball game we were watching, I heard my two kids make a call before the ref did. When a player was open, I heard them say, "Shoot, Shoot!" This tells me they not only are watching but also playing the game from the stands. This can give them a huge advantage when they actually step on the court.

Also, put your kids in a training environment around other athletes who are working at a high level. This will allow your child to not only raise their level of play but also allow them to see where they are as a player. More importantly, you as a parent can see or even get feedback from the trainer where your child needs more work, which leads me right to my next topic. If your kid is around kids who don't play at a high level, please remove them. Here's why: when you put a kid who knows the game in with kids who do not:

- low-level players crowd the best player
- the best player has a high risk of getting injured
- it takes the fun out of the game for the best player when corrections are being made every second
- it is very frustrating for high-level player
- the high-level player may do things that are unrealistic and too easy. Parents, please take time to learn your kids' level of play and put them on the right team or age group. This also plays a huge role in their skill development and keeps their fun and love for the game strong.

CHAPTER 8

CONCLUSION

Remember, you're the parent, and your role in your child's sports development has a lot to do with your words and actions. Please take a strong look in the mirror. Trust me, you're not alone. I did, and now my kids are better off for it.

I hope this book helps you, now, get out there and enjoy your kids' play.

ABOUT THE AUTHOR

Jamal Merrell, a devoted husband and father of two young children, embarked on an illustrious athletic journey that began with a full athletic scholarship to Rutgers University in 2009.

As a three-year starter and captain of the football team, his leadership on and off the field was exemplary. Following his collegiate success, Jamal signed a free-agent deal with the Tennessee Titans, marking another milestone in his remarkable sports career.

Today, as he sits in the stands alongside his wife he channels his wealth of experience into guiding parents through the seven keys to being exceptional sports parents in the modern era.

Today, as he manages two Youth Flag Football leagues and sits in the stands with his wife he channels his extensive experience into guiding parents on the seven keys to being exceptional sports parents in the modern era.

Printed in the USA
CPSIA information can be obtained
at www.ICGtesting.com
CBHW060748210724
11802CB00034B/704